Leading through the Fire

A Leader's Companion to Called to the Fire

The Covenant Path™ Series

Rich Van Doorn

**For every leader who dares to guide others
through the flame.**

*You have shown that holiness is not taught from a distance,
but walked out in the heat of surrender.*

*May your faith remain steady when the fire burns hottest,
and may your life remind those who follow that the One who
refines also restores.*

Contents

Foreword   vii

The Covenant Path™ Series Map   xi

Introduction   xv

Leader Covenant & Commitment   xxi

How to Use This Guide   xxv

1. Session 1: A Kingdom of Priests   1
   *(Based on Chapter 1 of Called to the Fire and Week 1 of Walking in the Flame)**

2. Session 2: Called Out and Set Apart   8
   *(Based on Chapter 2 of Called to the Fire and Week 2 of Walking in the Flame)**

3. Session 3: Sacred Space, Sacred People   16
   *(Based on Chapter 3 of Called to the Fire and Week 3 of Walking in the Flame)**

4. Session 4: Fire on the Mountain   24
   *(Based on Chapter 4 of Called to the Fire and Week 4 of Walking in the Flame)**

5. Session 5: Strange Fire and False Worship   32
   *(Based on Chapter 5 of Called to the Fire and Week 5 of Walking in the Flame)**

6. Session 6: Covenant Identity in a Hostile Land   40
   *(Based on Chapter 6 of Called to the Fire and Week 6 of Walking in the Flame)**

7. Session 7: Holiness in the Everyday   48
   *(Based on Chapter 7 of Called to the Fire and Week 7 of Walking in the Flame)**

8. Session 8: Clean Hands and Pure Hearts   56
   *(Based on Chapter 8 of Called to the Fire and Week 8 of Walking in the Flame)**

9. Session 9: The Discipline of the Holy   63
   *(Based on Chapter 9 of Called to the Fire and Week 9 of Walking in the Flame)**

10. Session 10: The Church in Exile   71
   (*Based on Chapter 10 of Called to the Fire and Week
   10 of Walking in the Flame*)*

11. Session 11: Standing Firm at the Crossroads   78
   (*Based on Chapter 11 of Called to the Fire and Week
   11 of Walking in the Flame*)*

12. Session 12: Rebuilding the Altar   86
   (*Based on Chapter 12 of Called to the Fire and Week
   12 of Walking in the Flame*)*

13. Session 13: A Light to the Nations   93
   (*Based on Chapter 13 of Called to the Fire and Week
   13 of Walking in the Flame*)*

Epilogue   101

About the Author   105
Also by Rich Van Doorn   107

Foreword

When Leaders Step into the Fire

There is a difference between lighting a fire and walking into one.

Many talk about holiness; few dare to lead others through it. The calling to guide God's people through the refining flames of discipleship is not glamorous—it is sacred. It means standing close enough to the heat that others might find courage to do the same.

Fire has always marked the presence of God. It appeared at Sinai, where a trembling people heard His covenant voice. It fell on Carmel, consuming both sacrifice and shame. It descended again at Pentecost, resting on the heads of those who would turn the world upside down.

Each time, the pattern was the same:

God revealed Himself through fire, and His people were never the same.

To lead through that fire is to walk the same path as Moses, Elijah, and the apostles—those who discovered that divine flame is both terrifying and tender. It consumes what cannot remain and strengthens what must endure.

Holiness is not simply what God demands; it is who He is. When you guide others toward holiness, you are not inviting them to moral reform—you are inviting them to stand where God stands, to see as He sees, and to live as He lives.

This is not a guide for managing lessons. It is a companion for carrying presence.

Every page, every session, every prayer in this book is designed to help you do what the priests of old were called to do:

> to stand between heaven and earth,
> to rebuild the altars that time and apathy have
> broken,
> and to remind the people of God that fire is not
> their enemy—it is their inheritance.

Holiness was never about isolation from the world; it was about illumination within it.

A holy people are not removed from the culture—they are refined for it.

As you lead through the fire, you will find that the flames reveal as much about you as they do about those you teach. That is by design. Leadership in God's kingdom is never performed at a distance; it is lived in the proximity of the Presence.

There will be moments when you feel the heat of conviction, the ache of self-examination, or the exhaustion of carrying others through their refining season.

In those moments, remember: the God who lights the fire also walks in it.

He walked with Moses in the burning bush,
with Shadrach, Meshach, and Abednego in the furnace,
and with His Church at Pentecost.
He will walk with you now.

"When you walk through the fire, you shall not be burned,
and the flame shall not consume you."

— Isaiah 43:2

May this guide strengthen your hands for holy work, steady your heart for sacred leadership, and remind you that the fire you carry is not meant to destroy—it is meant to define.

You are not merely a facilitator.
You are a keeper of the flame.

Lead well. Burn bright. And remember: every time you lead someone closer to the holiness of God, you stand again on holy ground.

The Covenant Path™ Series Map

Walking the Way of the Rabbi
— One Book, One Step at a Time

Your Journey Has Begun...

This Leader Guide — *Leading through the Fire* — is the next step in a 17-book discipleship journey.

Each book in *The Covenant Path™* series is paired with:

- A **Core Book** – Theological and historical foundations
- A **Devotional** – Six-day spiritual practice + Sabbath reflection
- A **Leader Guide** – Cultural insights, Hebraic terms, and small group support

* * *

THE COVENANT PATH™ SERIES (CONFIRMED TITLES & SUBTITLES)

1. **Dustprints of the Rabbi**: *Discipleship in the Texture of Torah and Grace*

2. **Hear, O Israel**: *Living the Shema in a World of Competing Voices*

3. **Called to the Fire**: *Becoming a Holy People in a Culture of Blending*

4. **Kingdom Beyond the Jordan**: *The Mission of Jesus in the Places We Fear to Go*

5. **Crimson Covenant**: *From Passover to the Cross and the Blood That Bought Us*

6. **The Cup and the Cry**: *Gethsemane, Judgment, and the Obedience That Redeems*

7. **Streams Beneath the Sand**: *Finding Presence and Provision in Wilderness Seasons*

8. **Strong and Shattered**: *What Samson Taught Us About Misused Strength and Second Chances*

9. **Shade for the Scorched**: *Shelter in the Midday Heat of Life's Hardest Days*

10. **Rooted in the Wind**: *Resilience, Trust, and the Torah of the Desert*

11. **Psalms from the Edge**: *Songs of the Wilderness, Hope, and the Haunted Heart*

12. **Voice Like a Shofar**: *Calling Out to God in Praise, Protest, and Prophetic Hope*

13. **Every Line a Return**: *Praying Our Way Back to Covenant*

14. **When Thrones Collide**: *Living Allegiant to the King in a World of Caesar*

15. **Corinth Wasn't Ready**: *Confronting Compromise in the Church and the City*

16. **Dwelling Among Us**: *Becoming the Temple God Meant to Fill*

17. **The Exodus Still Echoes**: *How God's Rescue Story Keeps Repeating Through Us*

* * *

HOW TO KEEP WALKING

Each step includes:

- A teaching book
- A companion devotional
- A leader guide like this one

Start with the next title — or gather a new group to walk through this one again.

Discipleship is not a class. It's a path. The Rabbi is still walking. So must we.

Introduction

Leading in the Fire

Leadership has always been forged in the flame.

Throughout Scripture, when God called a man or woman to lead, He did not hand them a throne—He handed them a fire. Moses met it in a bush that burned without being consumed. Elijah saw it fall from heaven on Mount Carmel. Isaiah felt it touch his lips in purification. And at Pentecost, it rested upon the heads of those who would carry the Gospel to the ends of the earth.

Fire is both terrifying and tender. It consumes what cannot remain and refines what must endure. That is the calling of every leader who steps into God's presence: to be refined, not destroyed—to burn without burning out.

You have chosen to lead others through that same sacred process.

This guide, *Leading Through the Fire,* exists to help you shepherd people through the refining work of holiness—the process by which God removes the impurities of the world so His image can shine through His people again. It is not a manual for control or performance. It is a map for courage.

* * *

THE WEIGHT AND WONDER OF HOLINESS

Holiness is not perfection. It is proximity.

In Hebrew, the word *kadosh* (קָדוֹשׁ) means *set apart*—different in purpose, distinct in presence. Holiness begins when the people of God stop trying to blend into the world around them and start embodying the covenant that defines them.

As a leader, you are not just teaching holiness—you are *hosting it*.

You are creating spaces where others can encounter God safely enough to surrender and reverently enough to change.

That will mean walking through fire yourself. You cannot lead others into refinement you've refused to face. But you will also discover that fire reveals what teaching alone cannot—it exposes the true condition of the heart and illuminates the power of grace.

Holiness is not what separates us from the world; it is what sends us back into it differently.

* * *

YOUR ROLE AS A COVENANT LEADER

In *Called to the Fire*, we learn that God's purpose for His people has always been priestly—to stand between heaven and earth as a kingdom of mediators, reflectors, and servants.

To lead others through holiness is to step into that priestly posture:

- **You stand in the gap** between what is and what could be.
- **You remind people of who they are** when the world calls them by other names.
- **You carry the flame** into places that have forgotten how to burn.

You will not always feel ready for this. Neither did Moses. Neither did Isaiah. But readiness is not the requirement—*willingness is.*

God does not demand that you manage the fire. He asks only that you stay in it long enough to let Him work.

$$* \quad * \quad *$$

A HOLY PEOPLE IN A BLENDING WORLD

We live in a time where conviction often feels inconvenient and compromise feels normal. The fire of holiness exposes that. It purifies motives, clarifies truth, and restores courage.

This is why your role matters. The world does not need more polished communicators—it needs consecrated leaders. Men and women who have stood in the presence of God long enough to smell like smoke.

To lead through the fire is to remind people that holiness still matters, that integrity still witnesses, and that covenant faithfulness is not outdated—it's revolutionary.

"You are the light of the world. A city set on a hill cannot be hidden."

— *Matthew 5:14*

The world grows darker by the day, but the darker it gets, the brighter refined faith shines.

* * *

A FINAL WORD TO THE LEADER

This is holy work.

It will cost you comfort but grant you clarity.

It will burn away pretense but leave you pure.

It will test your patience but strengthen your faith.

Each session in this guide will give you structure and support, but only the Holy Spirit can give you fire. Invite Him into your preparation, your leadership, and your silence.

Remember: you are not merely *leading* through the fire —you are *learning* through it. Every question you ask, every story you hear, every tear that falls in your group becomes part of the refining process.

May you lead with humility.

May you burn with love.

And may you discover, as every priest and prophet has before you, that the fire of God never destroys what is surrendered—it only makes it shine.

"For our God is a consuming fire."

— *Hebrews* 12:29

Leader Covenant & Commitment
Walking in the Dust Together

"Whoever wants to be great among you must be your servant."

— Matthew 20:26

* * *

As a leader on The Covenant Path™, I commit to:

1. Walk Behind the Rabbi First

I will lead not from arrival, but from pursuit. I will walk behind Jesus — not just talk about Him. My leadership will flow from discipleship.

2. Create Space for Formation

I will foster environments where others can wrestle, wonder, listen, and grow. I will lead with grace, humility, and spiritual curiosity.

3. Honor the Hebraic Roots of Our Faith

I will approach this journey with reverence for the Jewish worldview of Jesus and the first-century context of His teaching. I will define terms, invite questions, and point others to the richness of Scripture in its original setting.

4. Uphold Unity and Confidentiality

I will protect the sacred space of group conversations. What is shared in the group stays in the group, unless there is a need for loving accountability or safety.

5. Practice What I Facilitate

I will not call others to a path I am unwilling to walk myself. I will engage the devotional, reflect on the book, and live out the truth I ask others to explore.

6. Pray Before I Plan

I will lead prayerfully, not just practically. I will ask the Spirit of the Rabbi to guide each session and each heart — including mine.

* * *

LEADER COVENANT AFFIRMATION

Name: _______________________________

Date: _______________________________

"Rabbi Jesus, I offer You my steps, my words, my silence, and my leadership. May I guide others only as I follow You. Let

my feet stay in the dust, and let those who follow me find You there.
Amen."

How to Use This Guide
Leading Through the Fire

This guide was created to equip you—not with scripts to follow, but with **sacred tools** for leading others through God's refining fire. *Leading Through the Fire* walks in step with both *Called to the Fire* (the core book) and *Walking in the Flame* (the devotional). Together, they form a complete discipleship journey for groups who want to live as a **holy people in a blending culture.**

Each of the **thirteen sessions** in this guide corresponds directly with a chapter from the book and a week from the devotional. As you lead, your role is not simply to teach concepts but to **model consecration**—to show what holiness looks like when it's lived out in grace, humility, and courage.

* * *

THE HEART OF THE GUIDE

Fire both **reveals** and **refines.**

This study is built on that truth. Each session helps

your group encounter God's holiness, wrestle with the call to distinct living, and respond with obedience and worship.

You will notice a rhythm that mirrors the ancient pattern of *meeting, hearing, responding, and walking—a* structure drawn from the Torah itself. Every element exists to help your group not just learn, but live the truth.

$$* * *$$

SESSION STRUCTURE

Each session includes the following elements:

1. **Focus Verse** – The central Scripture for reflection and discussion.
2. **Theme Summary** – A short overview capturing the heart of the chapter's message.
3. **Leader Objective & Refining Focus** – A guide to the session's spiritual aim and desired transformation.
4. **Opening Prayer & Shema Reading** – A moment of communal centering and covenant remembrance.
5. **Moment of Stillness** – A brief guided pause to prepare hearts for reflection.
6. **Grounding in the Dust (Cultural Insight)** – Hebraic context, historical background, or rabbinic reflection that deepens understanding.
7. **From the Core Book** – Connection points and teaching prompts from *Called to the Fire*.
8. **From the Devotional** – Parallel insights and testimonies from *Walking in the Flame*.

9. **Group Discussion: Fire & Formation Questions** – Thoughtfully layered questions designed to move from reflection to action.
10. **Dustprint Discipleship Challenge** – A tangible weekly application that carries holiness into daily life.
11. **Closing Prayer & Group Blessing** – A unifying conclusion and moment of commissioning.
12. **Leader's Prayer of Consecration** – A private reflection for you, the leader, after each session.
13. **Leader Notes** – Space for insights, names, needs, and follow-up points.

* * *

PREPARATION TIPS FOR LEADERS

- **Read the Core Chapter First.** Begin each week by reading the corresponding chapter from *Called to the Fire*. Highlight key insights or phrases that resonate with your group's current journey.
- **Engage the Devotional.** Reflect personally through *Walking in the Flame* during the week before you teach. The devotional will soften the soil of your own heart before you lead others.
- **Pray for Refinement, Not Perfection.** Your transparency will shape your group more than your eloquence. Lead as one who is being refined, not one who has arrived.

- **Guide, Don't Dominate.** Create space for others to share how God's fire is transforming them. Let the group's honesty invite transformation more than your instruction.
- **Anchor Everything in Covenant.** Remind participants often that holiness is not behavior management—it's relationship restoration. The fire doesn't just cleanse; it consecrates.

* * *

FOR GROUP LEADERS AND TEACHERS

Each group will move at its own pace. Some will linger in reflection; others will move quickly into application. Adjust as needed—but never rush the work of the Spirit.

Your responsibility is not to control the flame, but to **tend it.**

Keep the atmosphere of your gatherings rooted in grace and truth. Encourage questions, embrace silence, and celebrate even the smallest signs of obedience.

The fruit of this study will not be measured by attendance or discussion—it will be seen in transformation.

"The fire will not consume you—it will commission you."

Lead with that conviction.
You are not just walking others *through* the fire.
You are leading them *into* the presence that transforms.

Chapter 1

Session 1: A Kingdom of Priests

(Based on Chapter 1 of Called to the Fire and Week 1 of Walking in the Flame)*

FOCUS VERSE

"You shall be to Me a kingdom of priests and a holy nation."

— Exodus 19:6

Theme Summary

Before giving His people laws, God gave them identity. At Sinai, He called Israel to be a *kingdom of priests*—not to isolate themselves, but to represent Him among the nations. Holiness was never meant to distance them from the world but to distinguish them within it.

As leaders, we are called to guide others into this same priestly posture: to reflect God's presence in the ordinary, intercede for those who wander, and model what it looks like to live as a holy people in a blending culture. Leadership is priesthood in motion—standing in the gap between heaven and earth so others can see God's heart.

Leader Objective

By the end of this session, leaders should help participants:

- Understand holiness as relational identity, not moral achievement.
- See themselves as priests—those who stand before God for others.
- Recognize that the Church's distinctiveness is its greatest witness.

Refining Focus: *Help your group see that holiness is not separation from people—it's saturation with God's presence.*

* * *

OPENING PRAYER & SHEMA READING

"Lord of holiness and mercy, You have called us into covenant, not comfort. Teach us to lead others as priests who carry Your presence into every place we go. Amen."

Shema Reading

Shema Yisrael, Adonai Eloheinu, Adonai Echad.
Hear, O Israel: The LORD our God, the LORD is One.

— Deuteronomy 6:4

MOMENT OF STILLNESS

Invite the group to breathe deeply and imagine standing at the foot of Sinai.

The mountain trembles. Smoke rises. The air is thick with awe.

Then hear God's voice—not calling for perfection, but for presence.

> *"You will be My treasured possession. My priests. My people."*

Pause for 20–30 seconds before continuing.

GROUNDING IN THE DUST (CULTURAL INSIGHT)

In the ancient Near East, priests existed to maintain favor between gods and men. Israel's God overturned that expectation—He made the *entire nation* priestly.

Every household, every farmer, every craftsman was invited to represent heaven on earth.

The Hebrew word for priest, **kohen** (כֹּהֵן), literally means *one who stands*. The sages said, *"When the righteous stand in prayer, the world stands with them."* (Avot 5:1)

Priests did not flee from the world's needs; they stood within them.

As leaders, we "stand" for our people—not above them, but among them. When we lead prayerfully, serve humbly, and speak truth with compassion, we mirror the priestly rhythm God designed for His people.

FROM THE CORE BOOK — CALLED TO THE FIRE

In *Called to the Fire*, Chapter 1 opens with God's declaration of purpose at Sinai: His people were chosen not for privilege, but for participation. The mountain's fire symbolized His presence—dangerous to touch, but meant to dwell among them.

The chapter reminds us that identity precedes obedience. God didn't wait for Israel to prove worthy before He called them holy; He named them holy so they could learn to live it.

Encourage leaders to discuss how God's call to priesthood shapes our approach to holiness: not as striving for purity to earn favor, but as living in reflection of the favor already given.

FROM THE DEVOTIONAL — WALKING IN THE FLAME

Week 1 of *Walking in the Flame* teaches that holiness begins in belonging. God's fire is both refining and defining —it burns away false identity until we remember whose we are.

Leaders should ask:

- *How did your group members experience "refinement" this week?*
- *Where did the fire reveal something God wanted to restore, not remove?*

Invite honesty. Refinement is often uncomfortable, but the goal is always restoration.

GROUP DISCUSSION – FIRE & FORMATION QUESTIONS

Fire Questions (Refining Reflection)

1. *What does it mean to you that God defines identity before giving instruction?*
2. *How does this challenge the way many Christians approach holiness?*
3. *When have you experienced refinement that ultimately revealed God's love, not His anger?*

Formation Questions (Practical Application)

4. *How can your small group function as a "kingdom of priests" for your community?*
5. *What does priesthood look like in everyday settings—home, workplace, ministry?*
6. *How can your leadership invite others closer to God instead of intimidating them away?*
7. *Where might God be calling you to "stand" in intercession this week?*

DUSTPRINT DISCIPLESHIP CHALLENGE

Ask your group to identify one tangible way to act as a priestly presence in their context this week:

- Praying for someone who's far from faith.
- Offering blessing instead of criticism.

- Bringing encouragement into a tense environment.

Leader Practice

Take ten minutes each morning this week to stand—literally—and pray silently for your group. Picture each person by name as you intercede for them.

Whisper: *"Lord, let me stand well before You for those You've entrusted to me."*

CLOSING PRAYER & GROUP BLESSING

Leader Prayer

"Holy God, You have made us a kingdom of priests—not to boast, but to bless. Refine our hearts to lead as You lead—with mercy, courage, and faithfulness."

Group Blessing

> *"May the fire of His presence rest upon you.*
> *May your lives reflect His holiness,*
> *and may the world see in you the light of the*
> *One who called you His own."*

Leader's Prayer of Consecration

> *"Refining Father, I surrender my need to*
> *impress and choose instead to intercede.*

Teach me to lead from the altar, not the platform.
Burn away fear, kindle faith, and let Your fire find a home in me. Amen."

LEADER NOTES

(Use this space for reflections, prayer requests, or follow-up insights from your group.)

Chapter 2

Session 2: Called Out and Set Apart

(Based on Chapter 2 of Called to the Fire and Week 2 of Walking in the Flame)*

FOCUS VERSE

"But you are a chosen people, a royal priesthood, a holy nation, a people for His own possession, that you may declare the excellencies of Him who called you out of darkness into His marvelous light."

— 1 Peter 2:9

Theme Summary

God's call to holiness is never a call to retreat—it is a call to represent. From Abraham's journey to Peter's proclamation, the story of Scripture reveals a God who draws His people *out* so He can send them *in*.

Holiness means being distinct, not distant. It's the art of carrying light into dark places without letting the darkness define you. Leaders must model what it means to live *set apart for mission*, not isolated from it.

The Church's witness suffers when holiness becomes performance instead of presence. True holiness is not about drawing lines—it's about drawing near, so others can see what covenant life looks like.

Leader Objective

By the end of this session, leaders should help participants:

- Recognize holiness as separation *for* mission, not separation *from* people.
- Identify areas where cultural blending has diluted distinct witness.
- Reclaim the call to be visibly different in character, compassion, and courage.

Refining Focus: *Help your group see holiness as transformation that moves outward—sanctified for service, not superiority.*

* * *

OPENING PRAYER & SHEMA READING

"Lord who calls and sends, thank You for bringing us out of darkness and into Your light. Teach us what it means to live set apart—not as spectators of holiness, but as bearers of it. Amen."

Shema Reading

Shema Yisrael, Adonai Eloheinu, Adonai Echad.
Hear, O Israel: The LORD our God, the LORD is One.

— Deuteronomy 6:4

MOMENT OF STILLNESS

Invite participants to reflect quietly:

"Picture the moment when God first called you—
when light broke through confusion or fear.
Remember how it felt to be chosen, not because you
were ready, but because He was faithful.
That same calling continues today. The God who
called you out now calls you forward."

Allow 20 seconds of silence before continuing.

GROUNDING IN THE DUST (CULTURAL INSIGHT)

In Hebrew, the word for "holy," **kadosh** (קדוש), literally means *set apart, distinct, other*. In rabbinic tradition, holiness is not defined by withdrawal, but by proximity to the divine purpose.

The Mishnah teaches:

"Where there is no holiness, there can be no mission; for the sacred draws the world toward its Creator."

— *Avot de-Rabbi Natan 11*

In Jewish culture, to be "set apart" was never a rejection of the world—it was the world's invitation to see what God is like. Israel was called to embody a different rhythm: mercy in conflict, justice in oppression, covenant in chaos.

As leaders, we help our groups see holiness not as what we leave behind, but what we *carry forward*.

FROM THE CORE BOOK — CALLED TO THE FIRE

In *Chapter 2*, the fire becomes personal. God calls His people out of Egypt's patterns and into His presence. But leaving Egypt is not just geographical—it's spiritual. The world's habits, idols, and fears still cling to the heart unless the fire refines them.

This chapter reminds readers that holiness is both a **departure** and a **destination**: leaving behind what enslaves in order to step into what sanctifies. Leaders should emphasize that the call to be "set apart" is not about superiority, but surrender.

Encourage discussion around this reflection:

"What still follows us from Egypt, and how is God calling us to lay it down?"

FROM THE DEVOTIONAL — WALKING IN THE FLAME

Week 2 challenges readers to live distinctively in the midst of blending culture. The focus verse (1 Peter 2:9) reminds us that holiness is not hidden—it's declared.

Encourage leaders to revisit the story from the devotional's *Day 4* (the firefighter who chose compassion in chaos). This story mirrors the priestly mission in modern form: staying in the fire long enough for others to see the light.

Ask your group:

- *What does it look like to live holy in your daily world without becoming self-righteous?*
- *Where do you feel called to bring light rather than escape heat?*

GROUP DISCUSSION — FIRE & FORMATION QUESTIONS

Fire Questions (Refining Reflection)

1. *What does "set apart" look like in your context— your work, home, or relationships?*
2. *How do we discern the difference between holiness and legalism?*
3. *Where have you experienced God calling you out of something that no longer fits who you're becoming?*

Formation Questions (Practical Application)

4. *How can your group model distinct living in a culture that blurs moral boundaries?*
5. *What daily habits help keep the "fire" of distinction alive?*
6. *How can we engage with the world without losing our spiritual integrity?*
7. *What "Egypts" still tempt us to return when the wilderness feels too hard?*

DUSTPRINT DISCIPLESHIP CHALLENGE

This week, invite each participant to identify one area where they sense God calling them to step out from the world's pattern—an attitude, habit, or compromise—and replace it with a covenant act of devotion.

Leader Practice

Spend one evening this week in intentional solitude. Ask the Lord:

"Where have I blended what You set apart?"

Journal what He reveals, and pray for the courage to make one visible change.

CLOSING PRAYER & GROUP BLESSING

Leader Prayer

> *"God who calls us out and sets us apart,*
>   *thank You for never calling us alone.*
> *Help us lead others with humility and*
>   *boldness.*
> *May our distinction bring You glory, not us*
>   *attention."*

Group Blessing

> *"May the light of His holiness rest upon you.*
> *May you walk boldly in the calling that*
>   *makes you different.*
> *And may your life remind the world what it*
>   *means to belong to the Holy One."*

Leader's Prayer of Consecration

> *"Lord, refine my motives. Let me lead*
>   *without pride, serve without fear, and*
>   *walk without compromise.*
> *May the fire that purifies me become the*
>   *light that guides others. Amen."*

LEADER NOTES

(Use this space for reflections, follow-up ideas, or prayer needs from your group.)

Chapter 3

Session 3: Sacred Space, Sacred People

(Based on Chapter 3 of Called to the Fire and Week 3 of Walking in the Flame)*

FOCUS VERSE

"Do you not know that you are God's temple and that God's Spirit dwells in you?"

— 1 Corinthians 3:16

Theme Summary

When God revealed His presence at Sinai, the mountain became sacred. Later, His presence filled the Tabernacle, and then the Temple. But through the Messiah, sacred space moved again—from stone to spirit, from structure to soul.

The holiness of God no longer dwells in walls but within His people. Every believer becomes a living sanctuary, carrying divine presence into homes, workplaces, and neighborhoods.

As leaders, our calling is to help people realize that holiness doesn't end when they leave a church building—it begins when they do. Sacred space is not defined by address but by awareness.

Leader Objective

By the end of this session, leaders should help participants:

- Recognize themselves as sacred spaces indwelt by God's Spirit.
- Understand that holiness flows outward into daily environments.
- Practice awareness of God's presence in ordinary moments.

Refining Focus: *Help your group see that sacredness is not found in places, but in people filled with God's presence.*

* * *

OPENING PRAYER & SHEMA READING

"Lord who fills the heavens and yet chooses to dwell within us, make us aware of Your presence. Teach us to lead as those who carry sacred fire into every place we step. Amen."

Shema Reading

Shema Yisrael, Adonai Eloheinu, Adonai Echad.

Rich Van Doorn

> *Hear, O Israel: The LORD our God, the LORD is One.*
>
> — Deuteronomy 6:4

MOMENT OF STILLNESS

Invite participants to sit quietly and place a hand over their heart.

> *"This is your sanctuary.*
> *Not because of what you've done, but because of*
> *Who lives within you.*
> *Breathe deeply and let that truth settle:*
> *The fire of Sinai now burns within the hearts of*
> *God's people."*

Pause for 30 seconds before continuing.

GROUNDING IN THE DUST (CULTURAL INSIGHT)

In the ancient world, "sacred space" meant proximity to the divine. Temples were viewed as the dwelling places of gods —mountains or man-made sanctuaries where heaven and earth met.

But Israel's story was different. God's presence didn't remain locked behind stone walls—it traveled in a tent, a *mishkan* (מִשְׁכָּן), a movable dwelling that mirrored His people's journey. Later, the prophets foresaw a time when God would dwell not in temples made by hands, but in hearts made holy.

The rabbis said, *"When two sit and speak of Torah, the Shekhinah rests between them."* (Avot 3:2)

Holiness was never meant to be static—it was meant to move.

Leaders today carry the same calling: to help believers become "mobile sanctuaries" where others can encounter God's presence.

FROM THE CORE BOOK – CALLED TO THE FIRE

In Chapter 3, we learn that sacredness is both proximity and purpose. God's people are called to *embody* His presence, not just visit it. When the fire of God dwells within, ordinary spaces become extraordinary.

The chapter traces the progression from Sinai to the Temple to the indwelling Spirit, showing that God's desire has always been to dwell *with* and *within* His people. Encourage your group to see holiness as habitation, not performance.

Reflection prompt: *"Where has God's presence made an ordinary place in your life sacred?"*

FROM THE DEVOTIONAL – WALKING IN THE FLAME

Week 3's devotional explores how holiness transforms both being and doing. One of the week's reflections highlights the modern parallel of a nurse who quietly prays over patients while cleaning hospital rooms. Her work became worship, not because of its visibility, but because of her awareness of God's presence.

Encourage your group to share similar stories—

moments where divine presence made the mundane meaningful.

Ask: *What happens when we stop trying to bring God into our world and start recognizing He's already there?*

GROUP DISCUSSION – FIRE & FORMATION QUESTIONS

Fire Questions (Refining Reflection)

1. *How do you define "holy space"? Has that definition changed over time?*
2. *What makes a person or place sacred in God's eyes?*
3. *When have you sensed God's presence most clearly in an unexpected place?*

Formation Questions (Practical Application)

4. *How can you lead your family, students, or coworkers to sense sacredness in ordinary moments?*
5. *What might change in your daily rhythm if you viewed every environment as an extension of God's dwelling?*
6. *How can we resist compartmentalizing faith— worship here, work there, rest somewhere else?*
7. *What spiritual practices help you stay aware of His presence throughout the day?*

DUSTPRINT DISCIPLESHIP CHALLENGE

Encourage your group to choose one ordinary space this week—a classroom, kitchen, office, or vehicle—and dedicate it as a sacred space. Pray over it daily, inviting God to make His presence known there.

LEADER PRACTICE

Each morning, whisper this prayer before beginning your day:

"Lord, wherever my feet stand, let Your presence dwell."

Keep a short note or journal entry about moments you became aware of His nearness.

CLOSING PRAYER & GROUP BLESSING

Leader Prayer

"Holy God, You have chosen to dwell in fragile vessels. Teach us to lead and live as temples of Your presence. Let every conversation, every act of love, every breath become worship."

Group Blessing

"May you go from this place as living sanc-
tuaries.
May the world see in you a light that trans-
forms ordinary ground into holy
ground."

Leader's Prayer of Consecration

"Refining Father, cleanse my heart, renew
my mind, and fill me with Your
presence.
Make me a faithful keeper of sacred space,
and let the fire within me illuminate every
step I take. Amen."

LEADER NOTES

(Use this space to record reflections, insights, or ways your group experienced God's presence this week.)

Chapter 4

Session 4: Fire on the Mountain

(Based on Chapter 4 of Called to the Fire and Week 4 of Walking in the Flame)*

FOCUS VERSE

"Now Mount Sinai was wrapped in smoke because the LORD had descended on it in fire; the smoke of it went up like the smoke of a kiln, and the whole mountain trembled greatly."

— Exodus 19:18

Theme Summary

The fire on Sinai was not a threat—it was an invitation.

Israel trembled at the sound, but God was drawing near. In the fire, He revealed His character: holy, merciful, and faithful. The people were meant to come closer, not run away.

As leaders, we stand in that same tension. We guide

others toward a God who is both approachable and awe-inspiring. The "fire on the mountain" reminds us that true encounter with God burns away comfort while revealing calling.

To stand before this kind of fire is to realize: holiness is not safe, but it is good.

Leader Objective

By the end of this session, leaders should help participants:

- Understand the fire as a revelation of God's character, not punishment.
- See that fear and reverence can coexist in authentic worship.
- Cultivate awe without distance and intimacy without presumption.

Refining Focus: *Help your group see that holiness is not found in comfort, but in the courage to draw near.*

* * *

OPENING PRAYER & SHEMA READING

"God of fire and mercy, You draw near in power and love. As we lead others to Your presence, help us to do so with reverence, humility, and hope. May our awe never become avoidance. Amen."

Shema Reading

Shema Yisrael, Adonai Eloheinu, Adonai Echad.
  Hear, O Israel: The LORD our God, the LORD is One.

— Deuteronomy 6:4

MOMENT OF STILLNESS

Invite the group to close their eyes.

> *"Imagine the mountain before you—smoke*
>   *rising, thunder echoing, light flashing*
>   *across the sky.*
> *You hear your name in the wind.*
> *You sense both fear and longing.*
> *This is the God who calls you closer."*

Pause for 30 seconds of silence before continuing.

GROUNDING IN THE DUST (CULTURAL INSIGHT)

In ancient covenant ceremonies, fire symbolized divine presence and purification. To the people of the ancient Near East, mountains were seen as meeting places between heaven and earth—natural temples where gods revealed themselves.

At Sinai, the true God revealed Himself not through idols or images but through *voice and fire*. The Midrash teaches, *"The voice of the Holy One divided into seventy tongues so that every nation might hear."* (Exodus Rabbah 5:9)

This was not a private revelation—it was a public calling. God's holiness was never meant to be hoarded; it was meant to be heard.

As leaders, we remind our groups that awe is not meant to paralyze; it's meant to propel. The mountain that burns becomes the place from which we are sent.

FROM THE CORE BOOK – CALLED TO THE FIRE

Chapter 4 paints the fire at Sinai as both terrifying and transformative. The people's fear caused them to shrink back, but Moses stepped forward. Leadership is often defined in that very moment—the choice to draw near when others retreat.

Encourage discussion around Moses' posture: he *entered the thick darkness where God was. (Exodus 20:21)* Leaders must learn to enter mystery, to trust the God whose presence both refines and restores.

Reflection Prompt: *"What does drawing near look like for you when God feels overwhelming?"*

FROM THE DEVOTIONAL – WALKING IN THE FLAME

Week 4 invites readers to rediscover reverence in an age that has grown casual with the holy. The devotional's *Day 3* reflection quotes the Mishnah:

"Where there is no reverence, there is no wisdom."

— Avot 3:11

Encourage participants to share where reverence has deepened their relationship with God, or where comfort has dulled it.

Invite honesty around the question: *Do we still tremble when the Holy One speaks?*

Remind leaders: *trembling is not weakness—it's worship.*

GROUP DISCUSSION – FIRE & FORMATION QUESTIONS

Fire Questions (Refining Reflection)

1. *Why do you think God chose fire to reveal Himself at Sinai?*
2. *What's the difference between healthy fear and destructive fear?*
3. *How do awe and intimacy coexist in your relationship with God?*

Formation Questions (Practical Application)

4. *How can we reintroduce reverence into modern worship without becoming rigid?*
5. *In what ways can leaders demonstrate awe through humility, not spectacle?*
6. *How do you lead others into God's presence when they're afraid of change or conviction?*

7. *What does it look like to stand firm when others pull back from the fire?*

DUSTPRINT DISCIPLESHIP CHALLENGE

Encourage your group to spend intentional time this week in quiet prayer—no requests, no lists—just reverence. Light a candle as a reminder of God's holiness, and sit in silence for five minutes each day.

Leader Practice

Set aside one morning or evening for worship without words. Simply listen.

Pray:

> *"Lord, teach me to approach You not as a concept to master, but a Presence to revere."*

CLOSING PRAYER & GROUP BLESSING

Leader Prayer

> *"Holy Fire, burn away our pride and purify our awe.*
> *Teach us to draw near with trembling joy.*
> *May our reverence reveal Your reality to the world."*

Group Blessing

*"May you go forth with courage to climb the
mountain of God.
May awe become your strength and reverence your rhythm."*

Leader's Prayer of Consecration

*"Lord, I stand where the mountain meets the
flame.
Burn away my comfort.
Kindle wonder again.
Let those I lead see in me a heart that fears
You rightly and loves You deeply.
Amen."*

LEADER NOTES

(Record moments of revelation or insight from your group. What stirred awe? What sparked courage?)

Chapter 5

Session 5: Strange Fire and False Worship

(Based on Chapter 5 of Called to the Fire and Week 5 of Walking in the Flame)*

FOCUS VERSE

"And Nadab and Abihu, the sons of Aaron, each took his censer and put fire in it and laid incense on it and offered unauthorized fire before the LORD, which He had not commanded them. And fire came out from before the LORD and consumed them."

— Leviticus 10:1–2

Theme Summary

Worship is sacred, not because of our passion, but because of God's presence.

Nadab and Abihu learned this the hard way. They brought their own fire—an imitation of holiness—and the result was destruction, not devotion.

The tragedy of "strange fire" still speaks today. Whenever we offer God something that looks holy but is rooted in pride, performance, or presumption, the flame turns dangerous.

As leaders, we must help our groups rediscover the humility that keeps fire pure. True worship burns only when God Himself lights the flame.

Leader Objective

By the end of this session, leaders should help participants:

- Understand that genuine worship begins with obedience, not creativity.
- Identify areas where zeal has replaced submission.
- Cultivate discernment between true passion and self-driven fire.

Refining Focus: *Help your group see that worship without obedience is fire without fuel—it burns hot but dies fast.*

* * *

OPENING PRAYER & SHEMA READING

"Lord of the true flame, cleanse our motives and our worship.
Where we've brought our own fire, forgive us.
Ignite within us what only You can sustain. Amen."

Shema Reading

Shema Yisrael, Adonai Eloheinu, Adonai Echad.
Hear, O Israel: The LORD our God, the LORD is One.

— *Deuteronomy 6:4*

MOMENT OF STILLNESS

Invite participants to sit in quiet reflection.

> *"Picture a priest holding a censer, trembling*
> *before the altar.*
> *The difference between holy fire and strange*
> *fire is not in the heat—it's in the source.*
> *Ask yourself: what flame am I carrying?"*

Pause for 20–30 seconds.

GROUNDING IN THE DUST (CULTURAL INSIGHT)

In Leviticus, fire symbolized the ongoing presence of God. The altar fire was never to go out because it originated from heaven itself (*Leviticus 9:24*). When Nadab and Abihu offered "strange fire," they ignored the pattern of holiness— they lit their own flame, bypassing the altar of obedience.

Jewish commentary in the *Sifra* notes:

> *"They sought to add love to the command, but love without command is destruction."*

Their intentions were emotional, not evil—but worship divorced from instruction becomes idolatry of self.

In Hebrew thought, holiness always begins with *submission to divine order.* Leaders, therefore, must help their groups understand that zeal is not the same as faithfulness. The difference between strange fire and holy flame is obedience.

FROM THE CORE BOOK – CALLED TO THE FIRE

Chapter 5 confronts the modern forms of false worship: when performance overshadows presence, when emotion replaces obedience, or when convenience replaces covenant.

The fire of God does not validate us—it purifies us. It calls us back to humility. In the book, the author reminds us: *"The altar was never meant to showcase talent; it was meant to reveal truth."*

Encourage your group to reflect on areas where worship might have become self-centered—where ministry has become about applause rather than offering.

Reflection Prompt:*"What areas of my worship need to be relit by God's own flame?"*

FROM THE DEVOTIONAL – WALKING IN THE FLAME

Week 5 challenges readers to examine the heart behind their offerings. One of the reflections quotes the Talmud:

"The purest incense is the heart that trembles when offered."

— Berakhot 17a

Encourage leaders to remind participants that trembling is not fear—it's reverence. When our hearts tremble rightly, our worship burns purely.

Ask your group:

- *What are modern examples of "strange fire"?*
- *How can sincerity still go astray if not aligned with God's direction?*

GROUP DISCUSSION – FIRE & FORMATION QUESTIONS

Fire Questions (Refining Reflection)

1. *Why do you think God responded so strongly to Nadab and Abihu?*
2. *What do their actions teach us about the difference between passion and pride?*
3. *How might well-meaning believers unintentionally bring "strange fire" today?*

Formation Questions (Practical Application)

4. *How can your group cultivate worship that flows from obedience rather than emotion alone?*
5. *What practical steps can we take to ensure our ministries stay centered on God's command, not human creativity?*

6. *How can we guard against burnout by letting God be the firekeeper, not us?*
7. *How can we restore humility and submission in our approach to worship and leadership?*

DUSTPRINT DISCIPLESHIP CHALLENGE

Encourage your group to pray before every act of service this week:

"Lord, light this fire Yourself."

Ask them to pause before leading, speaking, or serving—to ensure what they offer comes from the altar of His presence, not their own ambition.

Leader Practice

Each morning, whisper this prayer before ministry or work:

*"Lord, let the fire on Your altar never go out,
and never let me bring my own."*

Journal any shifts you sense in your spirit when your actions begin with surrender.

CLOSING PRAYER & GROUP BLESSING

Leader Prayer

"Holy Fire, forgive us for the times we've
tried to carry You in our own strength.
Rekindle the flame You began.
Let our worship rise from obedience, not
pride."

Group Blessing

"May your worship burn with purity, not
performance.
May your service be shaped by obedience,
not opinion.
And may the God who lights the true flame
keep your altar burning."

Leader's Prayer of Consecration

"Refining Lord, strip away the motives that
compete with Your glory.
Light in me only what You ignite.
Teach me to discern between my passion and
Your presence.
I choose Your fire, not mine. Amen."

LEADER NOTES

(Record insights, confessions, or moments where your group recognized areas of misplaced zeal.)

Chapter 6

Session 6: Covenant Identity in a Hostile Land

(Based on Chapter 6 of Called to the Fire and Week 6 of Walking in the Flame)*

FOCUS VERSE

"But Daniel resolved that he would not defile himself with the king's food, or with the wine that he drank."

— Daniel 1:8

Theme Summary

Holiness is most visible when faith meets pressure. Daniel's life in Babylon shows that covenant identity doesn't dissolve in exile — it deepens. He didn't resist culture by hiding; he did it by remembering who he was.

Every generation of God's people faces its own Babylon — a culture that demands compromise, conformity, or silence. Leaders must help their groups navigate that tension with courage, humility, and hope.

Holiness is not hostility. It's the quiet, steady refusal to forget who you belong to.

Leader Objective

By the end of this session, leaders should help participants:

- Recognize the difference between engaging culture and imitating it.
- Strengthen their covenant identity through daily practices of remembrance.
- Lead others with grace and conviction, even under pressure.

Refining Focus: *Help your group see that holiness is not rebellion against culture — it's reflection of covenant in culture.*

* * *

OPENING PRAYER & SHEMA READING

"God of exile and promise, teach us to stand firm without growing hard, to remain distinct without growing distant. Give us the courage of Daniel and the compassion of Christ. Amen."

Shema Reading

Shema Yisrael, Adonai Eloheinu, Adonai Echad.

Hear, O Israel: The LORD our God, the LORD is One.

— Deuteronomy 6:4

MOMENT OF STILLNESS

Invite the group to close their eyes and imagine standing in Daniel's place — far from home, surrounded by idols, yet carrying the memory of covenant in your heart.

*"Holiness is not a place you reach; it's a
Person you remember.
The world around you may change, but the
One who called you remains."*

Pause for 30 seconds.

GROUNDING IN THE DUST (CULTURAL INSIGHT)

In the Babylonian exile, Israel's entire system of worship was dismantled. There was no temple, no altar, no visible flame. Yet holiness survived — not in structures, but in memory.

The Jewish sages later said, *"When Israel went into exile, the Shekhinah went with them."* (Megillah 29a) God's presence was not bound to Jerusalem; it traveled with His people.

Daniel's resistance wasn't defiance — it was devotion. By remembering covenant practices (dietary laws, prayer, worship), he maintained internal fire in a foreign land.

As leaders, we help others see that faith is most credible

not when culture affirms it, but when conviction costs something.

FROM THE CORE BOOK – CALLED TO THE FIRE

In Chapter 6, the narrative parallels Daniel's integrity with the Church's modern exile in a post-Christian age. Just as Babylon sought to rename Daniel (Belteshazzar), culture still tries to rename believers—defining them by trends rather than truth.

The book emphasizes that covenant identity isn't lost through persecution; it's lost through imitation.

Encourage discussion around this reflection:

"In what subtle ways does today's culture attempt to rename us, and how do we resist that without becoming hostile?"

FROM THE DEVOTIONAL – WALKING IN THE FLAME

Week 6 highlights the fire of faithfulness in exile. The devotional includes a story of a believer working in a corporate environment who refused unethical practices and faced ridicule but chose integrity over acceptance.

Ask:

- *Where do you see parallels between that story and Daniel's life?*
- *How does the Spirit empower us to live faithfully when obedience costs us something tangible?*

Encourage group members to share personal "Babylon moments" — situations where they've had to stand apart quietly but firmly.

GROUP DISCUSSION – FIRE & FORMATION QUESTIONS

Fire Questions (Refining Reflection)

1. *What does covenant identity mean in a culture that resists biblical values?*
2. *How do we discern when to adapt and when to resist?*
3. *What temptations of Babylon (comfort, recognition, success) are most dangerous to your walk with God?*

Formation Questions (Practical Application)

4. *How can your group live out holiness publicly without arrogance?*
5. *What spiritual practices keep your "inner fire" alive when external support fades?*
6. *How can leaders model conviction and compassion simultaneously?*
7. *Where might your workplace or community be your "Babylon" to bless?*

DUSTPRINT DISCIPLESHIP CHALLENGE

Encourage the group to choose one area this week where they can quietly demonstrate covenant distinction — integrity in business, gentleness in conflict, or prayer in public.

Leader Practice

Each morning, pray Daniel's prayer of resolve:

"Lord, I will not defile the flame You've placed within me."

Write the word *Remember* somewhere visible (desk, mirror, or phone background) as a daily reminder of identity.

CLOSING PRAYER & GROUP BLESSING

Leader Prayer

> *"Holy God, sustain us in a world that forgets*
> *You.*
> *Let our lives speak quietly but clearly of*
> *Your truth.*
> *Give us the strength to stand when others*
> *kneel to compromise."*

Group Blessing

> *"May you carry covenant courage into your*
> *Babylon.*
> *May the fire within you never bow to the*
> *wind around you.*
> *And may the Holy One who stood with*
> *Daniel stand with you."*

Leader's Prayer of Consecration

> *"Refining Father, keep me faithful when*
> *faith feels costly.*
> *Let the holiness of my heart outshine the*
> *hostility of my surroundings.*
> *May Your fire in me be my only identity.*
> *Amen."*

LEADER NOTES

(Use this space to record cultural pressures your group discussed and how each person plans to stand distinct this week.)

Chapter 7

Session 7: Holiness in the Everyday

(Based on Chapter 7 of Called to the Fire and Week 7 of Walking in the Flame)*

FOCUS VERSE

"Whatever you do, work heartily, as for the Lord and not for men."

—Colossians 3:23

Theme Summary

Holiness often hides in the mundane.

The same God who met Moses in fire also meets mothers in laundry rooms, teachers in classrooms, and leaders in the tension of daily life. The sacred isn't a destination—it's a discipline.

When God's Spirit fills ordinary space, ordinary acts become worship. The way we speak, serve, and respond becomes a living reflection of divine character. As leaders, we must help our groups recognize that holiness is cultivated not in grand gestures but in consistent obedience.

Leader Objective

By the end of this session, leaders should help participants:

- See daily faithfulness as sacred, not secondary.
- Recognize that God's presence transforms ordinary work into worship.
- Develop spiritual attentiveness throughout everyday routines.

Refining Focus: *Help your group see that holiness is not rare—it's rhythm.*

* * *

OPENING PRAYER & SHEMA READING

"Lord of all moments, teach us to find You in the ordinary.
Open our eyes to see that no task is too small to be holy when it's done for You. Amen."

Shema Reading

Shema Yisrael, Adonai Eloheinu, Adonai Echad.
Hear, O Israel: The LORD our God, the LORD is One.

— Deuteronomy 6:4

MOMENT OF STILLNESS

Invite the group to breathe deeply and reflect.

"Where did you encounter God this week?
Was it during prayer, or perhaps in the interruption you
didn't plan?
The holy often hides in the places we overlook."

Pause for 20–30 seconds.

GROUNDING IN THE DUST
(CULTURAL INSIGHT)

In Jewish life, the line between sacred and secular was never meant to exist. The Mishnah declares:

"Let every deed be done for the sake of Heaven."

— Avot 2:12

This meant that every act—eating, working, resting, teaching—could reflect God's holiness when done with awareness of His presence. The Hebrew concept of **avodah** (עֲבוֹדָה) captures this unity. It means both *work* and *worship*.

Holiness in Hebraic thought is not about escaping the world, but transforming it. The table becomes an altar, the meal becomes communion, and the workplace becomes a sanctuary.

Leaders must help their groups live with this awareness: holiness is not an event—it's a way of life.

FROM THE CORE BOOK – CALLED TO THE FIRE

In Chapter 7, the fire no longer blazes from mountaintops—it glows in the hearths of daily faithfulness. The book teaches that the truest mark of holiness is consistency. The same God who met Moses in smoke now meets His people in service, patience, and perseverance.

Encourage your group to discuss:

"Where has God asked you to be faithful when no one is watching?"

Remind them: it's not lesser worship—it's hidden holiness.

FROM THE DEVOTIONAL – WALKING IN THE FLAME

Week 7 tells the story of a police officer who prays before each shift, asking God to help him serve with integrity and gentleness. His badge becomes a reminder that every act of justice is also an act of worship.

Ask:

- *What are your "badges" of worship in the everyday?*
- *How does God use your profession, routines, and responsibilities as a crucible for holiness?*

Encourage participants to share small moments from their week that revealed God's presence in unexpected ways.

GROUP DISCUSSION – FIRE & FORMATION QUESTIONS

Fire Questions (Refining Reflection)

1. *How do you define holiness in practical terms?*
2. *When do you struggle most to see God in the ordinary?*
3. *What habits or attitudes dull your awareness of His presence?*

Formation Questions (Practical Application)

4. *How can your home, workplace, or community become a sacred space?*
5. *What would it look like to live every task as an act of worship?*
6. *How can leaders model joy and reverence in simple obedience?*
7. *What disciplines help sustain daily holiness—especially in routine or fatigue?*

DUSTPRINT DISCIPLESHIP CHALLENGE

Invite your group to choose one routine activity this week—driving, working, cooking—and dedicate it to God's glory. Before beginning, pray:

"Lord, I offer this act to You as worship."

Leader Practice

Practice *awareness prayers* throughout the day: short acknowledgments like, "You are here," whispered in different settings. Keep a daily record of where these reminders changed your attitude or perspective.

CLOSING PRAYER & GROUP BLESSING

Leader Prayer

> *"God of every breath and moment, make our ordinary lives extraordinary by Your presence.*
> *Let holiness flow through our work, our words, and our waiting. Amen."*

Group Blessing

> *"May you find the holy in the humdrum.*
> *May every step become sacred,*
> *and may your life reflect the quiet rhythm of God's holiness in motion."*

Leader's Prayer of Consecration

> *"Refining Lord, let me lead with authenticity.*
> *Let my life preach louder than my words.*
> *May I find You not only in the fire, but in the*

folding, the serving, and the silence.
Amen."

LEADER NOTES

(Use this space to jot down examples your group shared of finding holiness in the ordinary.)

Chapter 8

Session 8: Clean Hands and Pure Hearts

(Based on Chapter 8 of Called to the Fire and Week 8 of Walking in the Flame)*

FOCUS VERSE

"Who may ascend the mountain of the LORD? Who may stand in His holy place? The one who has clean hands and a pure heart."

— Psalm 24:3–4

Theme Summary

The mountain of God is not climbed with effort but with integrity.

Holiness begins where hypocrisy ends—when the outer life and the inner life agree.

"Clean hands" speak of action; "pure hearts" speak of intention. Together they form the mark of the mature disciple: one whose worship and works align.

As leaders, we are called not merely to model moral behavior, but to embody moral wholeness—to live unfragmented lives where our leadership flows from our sanctification.

Leader Objective

By the end of this session, leaders should help participants:

- Understand purity as inner integrity, not mere avoidance of sin.
- Pursue holiness that is consistent in both private and public life.
- Recognize repentance as an ongoing practice of renewal, not shame.

Refining Focus: *Help your group see that purity is not perfection—it's alignment.*

* * *

OPENING PRAYER & SHEMA READING

"Lord, cleanse our hands from self-reliance and our hearts from divided motives.

Teach us to serve from purity and lead from humility. Amen."

Shema Reading

Shema Yisrael, Adonai Eloheinu, Adonai Echad.

Hear, O Israel: The LORD our God, the LORD is One.

Rich Van Doorn

— Deuteronomy 6:4

MOMENT OF STILLNESS

Invite participants to close their eyes and open their palms upward.

"Imagine standing before the mountain of the LORD.
Your hands are empty—your heart exposed.

What needs to be released before you can ascend?"

Pause for 30 seconds of silence before continuing.

GROUNDING IN THE DUST (CULTURAL INSIGHT)

In ancient Hebrew worship, ritual purity symbolized readiness for encounter. Priests washed their hands and feet before entering the Tent of Meeting (*Exodus 30:18–21*). The act was not about physical cleanliness but spiritual preparation.

Rabbinic tradition connects purity with singleness of intent. The *Talmud* says:

"The pure in heart see every act as service before Heaven."

— Berakhot 17a

To the Hebrew mind, impurity was not simply about defilement—it was about *disconnection*. A pure heart is one whose motives are unified toward God's will.

As leaders, we must help others see that purity is not a fence—it's a flow. It restores relationship, clears vision, and makes the presence of God tangible again.

FROM THE CORE BOOK – CALLED TO THE FIRE

Chapter 8 teaches that holiness requires congruence. When David prayed, "Create in me a clean heart, O God" (*Psalm 51:10*), he wasn't asking for moral polish—he was asking for wholeness.

The book contrasts *performance purity* (looking holy) with *presence purity* (becoming holy). It's easy to wash hands for others to see; it's harder to purify motives only God will notice.

Encourage your group to discuss:

"Where does your outer obedience outpace your inner honesty?"

FROM THE DEVOTIONAL – WALKING IN THE FLAME

Week 8 features a story of a young EMT who faced a moral decision on the job—whether to cover a mistake or confess it. Her choice to tell the truth cost her comfort but preserved her integrity.

Her story illustrates that "clean hands" sometimes come from hands that tremble. Purity doesn't always feel peaceful at first—but it leads to peace later.

Ask your group:

- What does a "pure heart" look like in real-world decisions?
- Where has honesty required courage in your own life?

GROUP DISCUSSION – FIRE & FORMATION QUESTIONS

Fire Questions (Refining Reflection)

1. What's the difference between purity and perfectionism?
2. How do you discern when your motives have drifted?
3. What areas of your life feel divided between image and reality?

Formation Questions (Practical Application)

4. How can your group create a culture of honesty and confession without judgment?
5. What practical habits cleanse the heart—prayer, journaling, fasting, accountability?
6. How can leaders model transparency without losing authority?
7. What role does repentance play in sustaining spiritual health?

DUSTPRINT DISCIPLESHIP CHALLENGE

Encourage your group to pray Psalm 139:23–24 each morning this week:

"Search me, O God, and know my heart; test me and know my anxious thoughts. See if there is any offensive way in me, and lead me in the way everlasting."

Leader Practice

Each night, perform a *handwashing prayer*. As you wash your hands, pray:

"Lord, cleanse my actions and purify my intentions."

Let that physical act remind you that inner holiness flows into outer living.

CLOSING PRAYER & GROUP BLESSING

Leader Prayer

"Holy God, align our hearts and hands so that our leadership reflects Your integrity.
Make us honest before You and humble before others.

*Purify our motives until all we desire is to
please You."*

Group Blessing

*"May your hands be ready to serve and your
hearts ready to love.
May you ascend the mountain of the Lord
with courage and return carrying His
peace."*

Leader's Prayer of Consecration

*"Refining Father, cleanse me from hidden
pride and quiet compromise.
Unite my heart to fear Your name.
May those I lead see not perfection, but
purity that points to You. Amen."*

LEADER NOTES

*(Use this space to record group reflections on integrity,
honesty, and inner renewal.)*

Chapter 9

Session 9: The Discipline of the Holy

(Based on Chapter 9 of Called to the Fire and Week 9 of Walking in the Flame)*

FOCUS VERSE

"Train yourself for godliness; for while bodily training is of some value, godliness is of value in every way, holding promise for both the present life and the life to come."

— 1 Timothy 4:7–8

Theme Summary

Holiness is not inherited; it's cultivated. The fire that refines must also be tended. Just as an athlete trains the body for endurance, the disciple trains the soul for obedience.

In every generation, the temptation is to confuse inspiration with formation. Moments of spiritual emotion are not substitutes for the discipline of daily surrender. The holy life grows where habit meets the Spirit's power.

As leaders, we model a disciplined holiness that is steady, sustainable, and Spirit-dependent—not self-manufactured perfectionism.

Leader Objective

By the end of this session, leaders should help participants:

- See discipline as devotion, not punishment.
- Understand that holiness requires intentional rhythms of practice.
- Develop small, repeatable habits that keep spiritual fire burning.

Refining Focus: *Help your group see that holiness is not a moment—it's muscle memory.*

* * *

OPENING PRAYER & SHEMA READING

"Lord who trains our hands for battle and our hearts for worship,

teach us to love the daily disciplines that draw us near to You.

Strengthen our resolve to keep tending the fire You've kindled. Amen."

Shema Reading

Shema Yisrael, Adonai Eloheinu, Adonai Echad.
Hear, O Israel: The LORD our God, the LORD is One.

— Deuteronomy 6:4

MOMENT OF STILLNESS

Invite participants to sit quietly and imagine their faith as a flame.

"Does it flicker from neglect or burn steady from attention? Holiness grows in the daily tending.

The hand that prays, the voice that forgives, the heart that returns again and again to the altar."

Pause for 20–30 seconds before continuing.

GROUNDING IN THE DUST (CULTURAL INSIGHT)

In Jewish life, discipline was woven into the daily rhythm of devotion. The Shema was recited morning and evening, prayers followed appointed times, and Sabbath rest was practiced weekly — not as duty, but as delight.

The Mishnah says:

"One who disciplines himself for the sake of Heaven finds freedom in every act."

— Avot 6:2

The Hebrew word for *discipline*, **mussar** (מוּסָר), means *instruction that shapes character*. It's not punishment —it's formation. Discipline in the Hebraic mindset means "to train through repetition what is true."

Leaders must help their groups reclaim discipline as worship: not drudgery, but the structure that sustains devotion.

FROM THE CORE BOOK – CALLED TO THE FIRE

Chapter 9 compares the life of holiness to the training of a priest and the perseverance of a soldier. Both require routine and repetition. The book reminds us that the sacred is sustained through structure—daily prayer, confession, Scripture, and silence.

It warns against emotional peaks with no follow-through: *"Fire that flashes without focus burns out quickly."*

Encourage your group to consider:

"What holy habits are missing from your routine, and what unholy ones have taken their place?"

FROM THE DEVOTIONAL – WALKING IN THE FLAME

Week 9 features a story of a martial arts instructor who spent decades refining the same foundational movements. When asked why, he replied, "Because mastery is in the repetition."

The devotional uses that metaphor to show that spiritual mastery is not learned in leaps, but in steps. We don't rise to the occasion—we fall back on our training.

Ask:

- *What daily disciplines sustain your faith when emotions fade?*
- *How do repetition and routine strengthen resilience?*

GROUP DISCUSSION – FIRE & FORMATION QUESTIONS

Fire Questions (Refining Reflection)

1. *How do you personally define "spiritual discipline"?*
2. *What is the biggest obstacle to consistent practice in your walk with God?*
3. *How does the culture's obsession with comfort challenge the discipline of holiness?*

Formation Questions (Practical Application)

4. What disciplines help you keep your spiritual fire burning steadily?
5. How can your group build accountability around shared practices?
6. How can leaders model discipline without becoming rigid or prideful?

7. How does the Spirit's grace empower effort without replacing it?

DUSTPRINT DISCIPLESHIP CHALLENGE

Encourage your group to choose one discipline this week—prayer, Scripture meditation, journaling, fasting, or rest—and commit to practicing it daily, no matter how short or simple.

Leader Practice

Pick one spiritual rhythm to strengthen this week.
Pray each morning:

"Lord, train me in Your ways until holiness becomes my habit."

Reflect on how structure creates space for Spirit.

CLOSING PRAYER & GROUP BLESSING

Leader Prayer

*"Refining Father, make us faithful in the small things.
When discipline feels dry, remind us that formation happens in hidden places.
Train our hearts to choose You again and again."*

Group Blessing

"May your routines become sacred,
your habits become holy,
and your fire never fade through neglect."

Leader's Prayer of Consecration

"Lord, I offer my patterns to You—my time,
my attention, my will.
Shape me through repetition until obedience
becomes reflex.
Let discipline deepen my devotion. Amen."

LEADER NOTES

(Use this space to record disciplines discussed by your group and insights about sustaining long-term faithfulness.)

Chapter 10

Session 10: The Church in Exile

(Based on Chapter 10 of Called to the Fire and Week 10 of Walking in the Flame)*

FOCUS VERSE

"Seek the peace and prosperity of the city to which I have carried you into exile. Pray to the LORD for it, because if it prospers, you too will prosper."

—Jeremiah 29:7

Theme Summary

The Church was never meant to be comfortable—it was meant to be consecrated.

Exile reminds us that home is not where we live, but Whom we serve.

In Babylon, Israel learned that holiness can flourish even when influence fades. God's people discovered that exile is not abandonment—it's assignment.

The same is true today. In a world that drifts further

from God's truth, the Church's role is not to retreat in fear but to represent Him in faith.

As leaders, we help our groups understand that exile is not loss; it's opportunity. It exposes false security and invites deeper dependence on the God who still reigns.

Leader Objective

By the end of this session, leaders should help participants:

- See exile as a context for mission, not despair.
- Recognize that holiness is tested and proven in cultural tension.
- Learn how to engage the world with conviction *and* compassion.

Refining Focus: *Help your group see that exile is not the absence of God—it's the arena of faith.*

* * *

OPENING PRAYER & SHEMA READING

"God of every generation and every nation, teach us to live faithfully in lands that do not recognize You.

Make us holy exiles—gentle, bold, and anchored in Your truth. Amen."

Shema Reading

Shema Yisrael, Adonai Eloheinu, Adonai Echad.
   Hear, O Israel: The LORD our God, the LORD is One.

— Deuteronomy 6:4

MOMENT OF STILLNESS

Invite your group to sit quietly for a moment.

*"Imagine standing in a foreign land—familiar faith,
unfamiliar culture.
You long for home, but the Spirit whispers: 'I am here too.'*

*Exile doesn't remove God's presence; it reveals your
dependence on it."*

Pause for 30 seconds of reflection.

GROUNDING IN THE DUST
(CULTURAL INSIGHT)

In ancient Israel, exile was both a punishment and a purification.

Removed from the Temple, the people learned that holiness could exist without location. The rabbis later taught, *"When Israel was scattered, the Torah became her sanctuary."* (Midrash Tanchuma, Noach 3)

They learned to pray without altars, to gather without priests, and to worship without walls. Out of exile came the synagogue, the prayer shawl, the daily rhythm of morning and evening devotion.

What felt like loss became innovation.

For modern believers, exile looks like spiritual marginalization—faith pushed to the fringes. But as in Babylon, God is not absent; He's reforming His people to thrive in the tension.

As leaders, we must teach that exile is not an interruption to God's mission—it *is* the mission field.

FROM THE CORE BOOK – CALLED TO THE FIRE

In Chapter 10, the Church is compared to Daniel's remnant—holy, hopeful, and unbending. The book challenges readers to embrace exile as an invitation to reflect God's glory where comfort once reigned.

It warns that nostalgia can become idolatry. The goal is not to rebuild the past, but to represent the kingdom in the present.

Encourage discussion around this reflection:

"How can we love the world without becoming like it?"

FROM THE DEVOTIONAL – WALKING IN THE FLAME

Week 10 tells the story of a nurse working in a hostile environment where faith-based compassion was ridiculed. Instead of withdrawing, she quietly lived out her values—listening, praying silently, and offering care without compromise.

Ask your group:

- *How does her story echo the call of Jeremiah 29:7?*
- *What does it look like to seek the peace of the city where you live?*

Encourage participants to view their neighborhoods, schools, and workplaces as places of holy exile—settings where the kingdom of God can still be revealed through faithful presence.

GROUP DISCUSSION – FIRE & FORMATION QUESTIONS

Fire Questions (Refining Reflection)

1. *What emotions do you feel when you think of the Church as being "in exile"?*
2. *How does God refine His people through seasons of cultural opposition?*
3. *What might we have to let go of to thrive as exiles rather than victims?*

Formation Questions (Practical Application)

4. *How can your group bless your community while maintaining biblical conviction?*
5. *What does faithful presence look like in a society that misunderstands holiness?*

6. *How can we teach younger believers to live with confidence instead of fear?*

7. *What are practical ways to "seek the peace of the city" this week?*

DUSTPRINT DISCIPLESHIP CHALLENGE

Encourage each group member to find one tangible way to *bless their city* this week—through service, generosity, or prayer.

Then **reflect:** *How does blessing those who oppose us reveal God's holiness?*

Leader Practice

Take a prayer walk in your local community this week. As you walk, whisper:

> *"Lord, this is still Your ground.*
> *Show me how to live as light in exile."*

CLOSING PRAYER & GROUP BLESSING

Leader Prayer

> *"Sovereign God, strengthen Your people to*
> *stand as holy exiles.*
> *Let our hope outshine hostility and our faith*
> *outlast fear.*

Teach us to love the world like You do—
fiercely and faithfully."

Group Blessing

"May you be faithful in exile,
steadfast in opposition,
and radiant in the ruins—
until the Kingdom comes in full."

Leader's Prayer of Consecration

"Refining Father, I choose to lead as one
sent, not stranded.
Help me to shepherd Your people with
courage in the unknown.
Make exile my altar and mission my fire.
Amen."

LEADER NOTES

(Use this space to note your group's reflections on living faithfully in a culture of exile.)

Chapter 11

Session 11: Standing Firm at the Crossroads

(Based on Chapter 11 of Called to the Fire and Week 11 of Walking in the Flame)*

FOCUS VERSE

"Stand by the roads, and look, and ask for the ancient paths, where the good way is; and walk in it, and find rest for your souls."

—Jeremiah 6:16

Theme Summary

Every generation faces a crossroads—a place where conviction and comfort collide.

At that intersection, holiness is revealed not through words but through decisions.

To stand firm in a culture that bends truth requires clarity, courage, and covenantal memory. The ancient paths are not nostalgic—they're enduring. God doesn't call us backward; He calls us deeper.

As leaders, our responsibility is to equip others to

78

discern the difference between standing still in fear and standing firm in faith.

Leader Objective

By the end of this session, leaders should help participants:

- Recognize moments of cultural and moral decision as opportunities for witness.
- Learn to stand firm in truth without arrogance or hostility.
- Anchor conviction in Scripture, not opinion or pressure.

Refining Focus: *Help your group see that conviction is not stubbornness—it's sacred loyalty.*

* * *

OPENING PRAYER & SHEMA READING

"Lord of truth and mercy, when the world sways, make us steady.

Teach us to discern, decide, and depend on You alone.

Give us courage to stand when compromise feels easier. Amen."

Shema Reading:

Shema Yisrael, Adonai Eloheinu, Adonai Echad.

Rich Van Doorn

Hear, O Israel: The LORD our God, the LORD is One.

— Deuteronomy 6:4

MOMENT OF STILLNESS

Invite the group to reflect silently.

"Picture a crossroads—the path of convenience to one side,
the path of covenant to the other.
Hear the Spirit whisper: 'This is the way; walk in it.'

What crossroads stand before you right now?"

Pause for 30 seconds before continuing.

GROUNDING IN THE DUST
(CULTURAL INSIGHT)

In ancient Israel, crossroads were sacred places of decision and danger. Travelers chose direction there—and so did prophets. Jeremiah stood at one such crossroads when Israel's leaders ignored God's voice, preferring smooth roads to straight ones.

The Midrash notes:

"When Israel forgot the paths of covenant, the prophets called them to remember the dust of Sinai."

— Midrash Tehillim 119

Standing firm at the crossroads requires remembering whose dust we follow.

In the Greco-Roman world, early believers faced similar choices—burn incense to Caesar or confess Christ as Lord. Their steadfastness wasn't defiance; it was devotion.

As leaders today, we teach that the ancient path is not the easiest—it's simply the one that still leads home.

FROM THE CORE BOOK – CALLED TO THE FIRE

In Chapter 11, the fire becomes a test of loyalty. The narrative recalls moments in Scripture when God's people stood firm at the edge of danger—Joshua at the Jordan, Elijah on Mount Carmel, Daniel before kings, and the early Church before empire.

The book reminds us: *"Faithfulness is proven not in seasons of peace, but at the pressure points of history."*

Encourage your group to discuss:

"What modern crossroads test your faith most—social, moral, relational, or professional?"

FROM THE DEVOTIONAL – WALKING IN THE FLAME

Week 11 features the story of a public school teacher who faced pressure to compromise her beliefs but chose instead to live quietly consistent—gracious, faithful, and unflinching.

Her witness reminds us that firmness does not always mean confrontation. Sometimes it's quiet consistency that defies compromise.

Ask:

- What does standing firm look like in your environment?
- How can firmness coexist with humility and love?

GROUP DISCUSSION – FIRE & FORMATION QUESTIONS

Fire Questions (Refining Reflection)

1. *What crossroads are you facing right now where faith and culture collide?*
2. *How do you discern when to speak and when to stay silent?*
3. *What fears make standing firm difficult for you?*

Formation Questions (Practical Application)

4. *How can your group encourage one another to remain steadfast in biblical conviction?*
5. *What practices or Scriptures anchor you when compromise seems easier?*
6. *How can leaders demonstrate conviction without alienation or pride?*
7. *What would it look like to choose the "ancient path" in today's world?*

DUSTPRINT DISCIPLESHIP CHALLENGE

Encourage each participant to identify one area where compromise tempts them—then take one clear step toward conviction.

Leader Practice

Each morning this week, pray:

> *"Lord, make me faithful at the crossroads.*
> *When the world turns, help me stand."*

Write Jeremiah 6:16 somewhere visible this week as a daily reminder of your calling.

CLOSING PRAYER & GROUP BLESSING

Leader Prayer

> *"Holy Lord, give us the strength of Daniel,*
> *the courage of Elijah, and the humility of*
> *Jesus.*
> *When we stand at the crossroads, may our*
> *choices echo eternity."*

Group Blessing

> *"May your convictions be clear and your*
> *compassion deep.*

Rich Van Doorn

May your steps stay true on the ancient path
that leads to rest for your soul."

Leader's Prayer of Consecration

"Refining Father, anchor me in truth.
Let my yes be yes and my no be no.
Make my leadership a compass that points
others to Your way. Amen."

LEADER NOTES

(Use this space to record areas of decision your group members are facing and how they plan to walk faithfully through them.)

Chapter 12

Session 12: Rebuilding the Altar

(Based on Chapter 12 of Called to the Fire and Week 12 of Walking in the Flame)*

FOCUS VERSE

"Then Elijah said to all the people, 'Come near to me.' And he repaired the altar of the LORD that had been thrown down."

— 1 Kings 18:30

Theme Summary

Before fire falls, the altar must be rebuilt.

Elijah's moment on Mount Carmel reminds us that revival doesn't begin with spectacle—it begins with surrender. When God's people return to the altar, His presence returns to the people.

The altar represents covenant restoration. It is the place where pride dies, forgiveness begins, and holiness is renewed. As leaders, we are called to lead others back to that place—not through guilt, but through grace.

86

Rebuilding the altar is not just a task; it's a turning.

Leader Objective

By the end of this session, leaders should help participants:

- Understand the altar as a symbol of covenant renewal and worship.
- Identify what "broken altars" look like in personal and communal life.
- Lead others into repentance and restoration with hope, not shame.

Refining Focus: *Help your group see that rebuilding the altar means returning to the relationship that fire was always meant to sustain.*

* * *

OPENING PRAYER & SHEMA READING

"God who rebuilds what we break, we come not to impress You, but to return to You.

Teach us to restore the altar of worship in our hearts and in our homes. Amen."

Shema Reading

Shema Yisrael, Adonai Eloheinu, Adonai Echad.

Hear, O Israel: The LORD our God, the LORD is One.

— Deuteronomy 6:4

MOMENT OF STILLNESS

Invite participants to bow their heads and reflect.

*"Picture the altar of your life—the stones of prayer,
obedience, and devotion.
Which ones are cracked? Which have been neglected?*

Hear the whisper: 'Come near to Me.'"

Pause for 30 seconds before continuing.

GROUNDING IN THE DUST
(CULTURAL INSIGHT)

In Elijah's day, altars were physical—places of encounter
and atonement. But in Hebraic thought, they symbolized
more than sacrifice; they marked *relationship*.

An altar was where heaven met earth, where covenant
was renewed through worship.

The sages taught:

"When the altar is whole, peace fills the land."

— Midrash Rabbah, Leviticus 9:9

Rebuilding the altar was an act of restoration, not ritual.
It declared that God's place in the community was central
again.

In modern discipleship, rebuilding the altar means re-centering our lives on God's presence—reordering priorities, confessing distractions, and renewing devotion. Leaders help their groups rediscover worship not as a weekly event, but as a daily posture.

FROM THE CORE BOOK – CALLED TO THE FIRE

Chapter 12 reminds us that Elijah didn't just confront false worship—he repaired true worship. The book draws a powerful parallel: before the Church can confront the idols of culture, it must restore the integrity of its own altar.

The fire of revival doesn't fall on appearance—it falls on alignment.

Encourage your group to discuss:

"What does rebuilding the altar look like in your own life, family, or ministry?"

FROM THE DEVOTIONAL – WALKING IN THE FLAME

Week 12 tells the story of a pastor who experienced burnout and disillusionment, only to rediscover God's presence through daily quiet surrender. He rebuilt his altar not in a pulpit, but in a prayer chair.

Ask your group:

- *Where has your altar been neglected by busyness or distraction?*
- *How can small acts of worship rekindle intimacy with God?*

Encourage transparency and grace. Rebuilding always begins with honesty.

GROUP DISCUSSION – FIRE & FORMATION QUESTIONS

Fire Questions (Refining Reflection)

1. *What are some modern "altars" that have been torn down—personally or in the Church?*
2. *Why do we often resist returning to them?*
3. *What does repentance mean to you in light of covenant renewal?*

Formation Questions (Practical Application)

4. *How can your group create sacred rhythms that rebuild the altar of worship together?*
5. *What steps can you take this week to restore what spiritual neglect has eroded?*
6. *How can leaders help others rebuild altars of prayer, rest, and gratitude in their homes?*
7. *What does it look like for fire to fall again in our generation?*

DUSTPRINT DISCIPLESHIP CHALLENGE

Encourage your group to physically create or renew a space of worship this week—a prayer corner, a journal, or even a small outdoor spot. Dedicate it as a personal altar where they meet with God daily.

Leader Practice

Before each day begins, pause to pray:

> *"Lord, restore Your altar in me.*
> *Let the fire of devotion never go out."*

Light a candle or kneel in a familiar place as a physical act of recommitment.

CLOSING PRAYER & GROUP BLESSING

Leader Prayer

> *"God of the altar, rebuild what we have*
> *neglected.*
> *Let Your fire fall again—not to destroy, but to*
> *dwell.*
> *Teach us to lead others to You, not through*
> *guilt, but through grace."*

Group Blessing

> *"May your altar be restored,*
> *your fire rekindled,*
> *and your worship renewed.*
> *May your life burn as a living sacrifice*
> *before the Holy One."*

Rich Van Doorn

Leader's Prayer of Consecration

*"Refining Father, teach me to lead from the
altar, not the platform.
Make me a builder of sacred places,
where Your fire finds room to rest. Amen."*

LEADER NOTES

*(Use this space to record moments of recommitment, repen-
tance, or restoration shared by your group.)*

Chapter 13

Session 13: A Light to the Nations

(Based on Chapter 13 of Called to the Fire and Week 13 of Walking in the Flame)*

FOCUS VERSE

"I will make you as a light for the nations, that My salvation may reach to the end of the earth."

— Isaiah 49:6

Theme Summary

The purpose of holiness is witness.

God refines His people not to isolate them but to illuminate the world through them. Every spark of transformation in a believer's life is meant to kindle hope in another.

When the fire on the altar becomes the fire in the heart, the world begins to see the glory of God reflected in His people.

This is the destiny of the covenant community: not to escape darkness, but to shine within it.

Leaders carry that torch. Their lives are living lamps, reminding others that holiness and mission are inseparable.

Leader Objective

By the end of this session, leaders should help participants:

- Understand that holiness culminates in mission, not maintenance.
- Recognize that God's light shines most clearly through refined lives.
- Embrace their identity as covenant witnesses in a blending world.

Refining Focus: *Help your group see that the purpose of fire is not perfection — it's projection.*

* * *

OPENING PRAYER & SHEMA READING

"Lord of light and nations, You have refined us not to remain still, but to reflect You.

Ignite in us a holy boldness to carry Your presence wherever darkness dwells. Amen."

Shema Reading

Shema Yisrael, Adonai Eloheinu, Adonai Echad.
Hear, O Israel: The LORD our God, the LORD is One.

— Deuteronomy 6:4

MOMENT OF STILLNESS

Invite participants to close their eyes.

"Picture the fire of God not on a mountain or an altar, but within your chest.
See that flame extend outward—into your family, your city, your nation.

The same fire that refines you also reveals Him."

Pause for 30 seconds.

GROUNDING IN THE DUST (CULTURAL INSIGHT)

In Jewish thought, Israel's calling was never inward—it was outward. From Abraham's covenant in Genesis 12 to Isaiah's prophecy in 49:6, God's plan was always to bless all nations through His people.

Rich Van Doorn

The *Midrash Rabbah* says:

> *"When Israel walks in holiness, the nations see the light of the Holy One through them."*

— Genesis Rabbah 60:6

This wasn't national pride; it was divine purpose. Holiness was never about exclusion—it was about revelation.

In the first century, Jesus echoed this same vision when He told His disciples, *"You are the light of the world."* The fire from Sinai found its fulfillment in tongues of flame at Pentecost.

As leaders, we now carry that legacy—the priesthood of believers, set apart to shine.

FROM THE CORE BOOK – CALLED TO THE FIRE

In Chapter 13, the focus shifts from Israel's covenant to the Church's commission. The book traces the arc from Sinai's fire to the Spirit's fire, showing that the same God who descended on the mountain now indwells His people.

Holiness becomes missional. It moves from temple to table, from worship to witness. The Church becomes the lampstand through which the world sees the radiance of the Redeemer.

Encourage discussion around this question:

> *"How can holiness and mission become one rhythm in our lives?"*

FROM THE DEVOTIONAL – WALKING IN THE FLAME

Week 13 ends the devotional journey with a story of a fire-fighter who, after years of service, recognized that every rescue was an echo of God's own saving heart. His courage reflected covenant compassion.

Ask your group:

- *How does your vocation or influence serve as a vessel for God's light?*
- *Where might He be calling you to shine next?*

Invite participants to see their ordinary spaces as sacred assignments.

GROUP DISCUSSION – FIRE & FORMATION QUESTIONS

Fire Questions (Refining Reflection)

1. *What does being a "light to the nations" look like in your everyday life?*
2. *How can holiness and mission remain balanced without one overshadowing the other?*
3. *What fears or hesitations keep you from reflecting God's light publicly?*

Formation Questions (Practical Application)

4. *How can your group live missionally as a community of holy presence?*
5. *What small acts of light can bring hope to dark places around you?*
6. *How do leaders help others see that holiness is for the world's sake, not self-image?*
7. *Where do you sense God sending you now as His representative?*

DUSTPRINT DISCIPLESHIP CHALLENGE

Encourage your group to intentionally bless someone outside their faith community this week—a neighbor, coworker, or stranger—through an act of compassion or service.

Leader Practice

Each morning, pray:

"Lord, let Your fire in me become light for others."

Then look for one moment each day to embody that light—through words, presence, or action.

CLOSING PRAYER & GROUP BLESSING

Leader Prayer

*"God of mission and mercy, send us out in
Your fire.
Let our lives burn bright in compassion,
conviction, and courage.
May the nations see Your light in our love."*

Group Blessing

*"May you carry the flame of holiness into a
world that hungers for light.
May your presence remind others of the One
who called you from the fire.
And may your life be His living lamp until
He returns."*

Leader's Prayer of Consecration

*"Refining Father, thank You for the journey
through the fire.
As I lead others forward, keep my flame pure
and my heart humble.
Make me a torchbearer of Your glory.
Amen."*

LEADER NOTES

(Use this space to record how your group plans to live missionally after this final session.)

Epilogue

Still in the Fire

You have stood where few choose to stand—between heaven's flame and humanity's frailty. You have guided others through the refining heat of holiness, through seasons of conviction, courage, and renewal. You have led not as one who commands from a distance, but as one who walks in the glow of the same fire that purifies your people.

Leadership in the Kingdom was never meant to be comfortable. It was meant to be consecrated. Like Moses, you have climbed mountains that tremble. Like Elijah, you have rebuilt altars long neglected. Like Daniel, you have held your identity steady in the midst of exile.

This journey through *Called to the Fire* was not about acquiring knowledge—it was about recovering sacred presence.

Every chapter you've taught, every prayer you've led, every tear you've witnessed has been part of a greater story: God reclaiming a holy people for Himself.

Holiness, at its heart, is not a list of restrictions but a rhythm of relationship.

And as you've led others to walk in that rhythm, the fire has shaped you too.

The Hebrew prophets often spoke of *refiner's fire* (מְצָרֵף, *metsaref*)—a heat that does not destroy but defines. They knew that the fire of God was never meant to consume His people; it was meant to clarify their purpose.

So too for you, leader of covenant people: the fire that tried you has also trusted you.

"The fire will test what sort of work each one has done."

— *1 Corinthians 3:13*

The work you have done here is holy work. Not flawless, not finished—but faithful. And faithfulness is what keeps the flame alive.

Carry this truth with you as you go:

You are not stepping out of the fire; you are carrying it with you.
Into your home.
Into your ministry.
Into every conversation, every act of mercy, every decision that requires courage.

When others see the light in your eyes, may they glimpse the reflection of Sinai's flame and Calvary's love— the same fire that called you, purified you, and now sends you.

"Arise, shine, for your light has come, and the glory of the LORD has risen upon you."

— *Isaiah 60:1*

The altar has been rebuilt.
The flame has been rekindled.
The holy work continues.

Walk boldly, priest of the covenant.
The world needs your fire.

About the Author

Rich Van Doorn is a disciple, teacher, and spiritual pathfinder committed to helping others walk in the dust of the Rabbi. With over four decades of experience in biblical study, martial arts instruction, and faith-based leadership, Rich blends Hebraic scholarship with practical discipleship to awaken a deeper, more covenantal walk with Jesus.

Rich serves as the founder of *The Covenant Path*™—a multi-volume series designed to restore the ancient rhythms of following Yeshua in a world that often forgets the cost. Deeply influenced by the teachings of Ray Vander Laan, Dr. Eli Lizorkin-Eyzenberg, and Dr. Kenneth Bailey, his writing reflects a passion for the Jewish roots of Christianity and the call to live out faith with fierce obedience.

He is also the Grandmaster and Head of School at *Saja Martial Arts*, a Christian martial arts program that trains students to embody courage, humility, and discipline under the banner of Proverbs 28:1: *"The righteous are bold as a lion."*

Rich lives with his wife Mary and their family in the United States, where their home is filled with faith, laughter, and the unshakable belief that every step matters when you walk the path of the Rabbi.

Also by Rich Van Doorn

THE COVENANT PATH™ SERIES

1. **Book 1: Dustprints of the Rabbi — Discipleship in the Texture of Torah and Grace**
   - **Walking in the Dust:** *A 14-Week Journey of Faith, Formation, and Following the Rabbi*
   - **Guiding in the Dust:** *A Leader's Companion to Dustprints of the Rabbi*
2. **Book 2: Hear, O Israel — Living the Shema in a World of Competing Voices**
   - **Listening in Love:** *A 12-Week Journey of Devotion, Obedience, and Covenant Wholeness*
   - **Leading with the Shema:** *A Leader's Companion to Hear, O Israel*
3. **3. Book 3: Called to the Fire — Becoming a Holy People in a Culture of Blending**
   - **Walking in the Flame:** *A 13-Week Journey of Holiness, Identity, and Sacred Courage*
   - **Leading Through the Fire:** *A Leader's Companion to Called to the Fire*
4. **Book 4: Kingdom Beyond the Jordan — The Mission of Jesus in the Places We Fear to Go**
   - **Crossing with Courage:** *A 13-Week Journey into the Mission of Jesus in the Places We Fear to Go*
   - **Leading Beyond the Jordan:** *A Leader's Companion to Kingdom Beyond the Jordan*

5. **Book 5: Crimson Covenant — From Passover to the Cross and the Blood That Bought Us**
   - **Walking the Crimson Path:** *A 12-Week Journey from Passover to the Cross and the Blood That Bought Us*
   - **Leading in the Crimson Covenant:** *A Leader's Companion to Crimson Covenant*
6. **Book 6: The Cup and the Cry — Gethsemane, Judgment, and the Obedience That Redeems**
   - **In the Garden with the King:** *A 12-Week Journey through Gethsemane, Judgment, and the Obedience That Redeems*
   - **Leading to the Cross:** *A Leader's Companion to The Cup and the Cry*
7. **Book 7: Streams Beneath the Sand — Finding Presence and Provision in Wilderness Seasons**
   - **Drinking Deep in the Desert:** *A 12-Week Journey of Presence and Provision in Wilderness Seasons*
   - **Leading to the Living Water:** *A Leader's Companion to Streams Beneath the Sand*
8. **Book 8: Strong and Shattered — What Samson Taught Us About Misused Strength and Second Chances**
   - **Strength Redeemed:** *A 12-Week Journey of Misused Power and God's Second Chances*
   - **Leading the Broken Strong:** *A Leader's Companion to Strong and Shattered*
9. **Book 9: Shade for the Scorched — Shelter in the Midday Heat of Life's Hardest Days**
   - **Rest in the Heat:** *A 12-Week Journey of Shelter in Life's Hardest Days*

- **Leading in the Shade:** *A Leader's Companion to Shade for the Scorched*
10. **Book 10: Rooted in the Wind — Resilience, Trust, and the Torah of the Desert**
    - **Roots That Hold:** *A 12-Week Journey of Resilience, Trust, and the Torah of the Desert*
    - **Leading Through the Storm:** *A Leader's Companion to Rooted in the Wind*
11. **Book 11: Psalms from the Edge — Songs of the Wilderness, Hope, and the Haunted Heart**
    - **Songs in the Wilderness:** *An 11-Week Journey of Hope, Healing, and the Haunted Heart*
    - **Leading from the Edge:** *A Leader's Companion to Psalms from the Edge*
12. **Book 12: Voice Like a Shofar — Calling Out to God in Praise, Protest, and Prophetic Hope**
    - **Hearing the Holy Sound:** *A 12-Week Journey of Praise, Protest, and Prophetic Hope*
    - **Leading with the Shofar:** *A Leader's Companion to Voice Like a Shofar*
13. **Book 13: Every Line a Return — Praying Our Way Back to Covenant**
    - **Lines Back to Love:** *A 12-Week Journey of Praying Our Way Back to Covenant*
    - **Leading the Return:** *A Leader's Companion to Every Line a Return*
14. **Book 14: When Thrones Collide — Living Allegiant to the King in a World of Caesar**
    - **King Above All:** *A 12-Week Journey of Allegiance to Jesus in a World of Caesar*
    - **Leading Through the Collision:** *A Leader's Companion to When Thrones Collide*

15. **Book 15: Corinth Wasn't Ready —
Confronting Compromise in the Church
and the City**
   - **Letters to a Compromised Church:** *A
   12-Week Journey of Confronting Compromise
   with Covenant Faithfulness*
   - **Leading in Corinth:** *A Leader's Companion
   to Corinth Wasn't Ready*
16. **Book 16: Dwelling Among Us — Becoming
the Temple God Meant to Fill**
   - **Temple of His Presence:** *A 12-Week
   Journey of Becoming the Dwelling Place God
   Meant to Fill*
   - **Leading God's Living Temple:** *A Leader's
   Companion to Dwelling Among Us*
17. **Book 17: The Exodus Still Echoes — How
God's Rescue Story Keeps Repeating
Through Us**
   - **Walking Free Again:** *A 12-Week Journey
   into God's Rescue Story That Keeps Repeating
   Through Us*
   - **Leading the Exodus People:** *A Leader's
   Companion to The Exodus Still Echoes*

* * *

MARTIAL ARTS WORKS

Warrior Spirit: *Incorporating Biblical Teachings into Your
Martial Arts Journey*

Covenant Warrior Adaptations

Including forthcoming titles such as expanded, covenant-rooted *adaptations of classical works like **The Art of War**, **The Book of Five Rings**, and **The Bubishi**, reimagined for the modern Christian martial artist.*